Trading Volume

Utilizing Trading Volume to Validate Market Trends and Entries

Abraham Robert. C

Copyright©2024 Abraham Robert .C

All Rights Reserved

TABLE OF CONTENT

CHAPTER 1 — 7

TRADING VOLUME — 7
VOLUME BY TIMEFRAME — 8
VOLUME BY PRICE — 9
VOLUME BUYING AND SELLING CLIMAXES — 9
Buying climax — 10
Selling climax — 10
CRUCIAL POINTS TO BETTER UNDERSTAND TRADING VOLUME — 11

CHAPTER 2 — 15

IMPORTANCE OF TRADING VOLUME IN INVESTMENT — 15
IDENTIFYING MARKET TRENDS — 17
ASSESSING LIQUIDITY — 17
CONFIRMING PRICE MOVEMENT — 18
IDENTIFYING POTENTIAL OPPORTUNITIES — 19
ENTRY AND EXIT — 19
MARKET DEPTH — 20
VOLATILITY MEASUREMENT — 20
IDENTIFYING BREAKOUTS — 21
CONFIRMATION OF REVERSALS — 21
DIVERGENCE ANALYSIS — 21

Risk management . . . 22

Investor sentiment . . . 22

CHAPTER 3 . . . 25

Factors affecting trading volume . . . 25

Economic Indicators . . . 25

News and events . . . 26

Market Volatility . . . 27

Market structure . . . 27

Investor participation . . . 28

Market liquidity . . . 29

Marketing Trends . . . 29

Regulatory changes . . . 30

Marketing Psychology . . . 30

Market exuberance . . . 31

Market microstructure . . . 31

Government policies . . . 32

Global events . . . 32

Market Accessibility . . . 33

Technological Advances . . . 33

Seasonal factors . . . 34

Market Speculation . . . 34

CHAPTER 4 . . . 35

VOLUME TRADING STRATEGIES — 35

SUPPORT AND RESISTANCE LEVELS — 35

BREAKOUT AND BREAKDOWN — 36

TREND STRENGTH — 36

VOLUME DIVERGENCE — 37

VOLUME REVERSAL — 38

HOW TO MEASURE TRADING VOLUME — 39

DETAILS ON TRADING VOLUME MEASUREMENT — 40

VOLUME BASED INDICATORS — 40

On-Balance Volume (OBV): — 41

Chaikin Cash Flow (CMF): — 41

Volume weighted average price (VWAP): — 42

Accumulation and Distribution Line (ADL): — 42

Money Flow Index: — 42

CHAPTER 5 — 45

TRADING VOLUME TIPS FOR SWING AND DAY TRADERS — 45

TRADING VOLUME TIPS FOR DAY TRADERS — 46

Look for strong trading volumes — 46

Analyze intraday volume patterns — 46

Use trade volume in combination with technical indicators — 47

Monitor news and events — 48

Identify the abnormal trading volume — 48

TRADING VOLUME TIPS FOR SWING TRADERS — 49

Volume Analysis of Entry and Exit	49
Identify volume patterns	50
Focus on liquid stocks or pairs	51
Volume Confirmation	51
Volume Surge at Breakouts	52
Volume Divergence	53
Volume Confirmation for Pullbacks	53
Volume at the Support and Resistance levels	54
Volume Patterns for Consolidation	55
Stay informed about news events	56
ADVANTAGES AND DISADVANTAGES OF ANALYZING TRADING VOLUME	56
The advantages	56
The disadvantages	57

CHAPTER 6   59

SUMMARY	**59**
TRADING VOLUME: KEY TO SUCCESS	59
Liquidity	59
Price movements	60
Confirmation	61
Risk Management	61

Chapter 1

Trading Volume

Trading volume is an important indicator of market activity that is closely watched by both traders and investors. Understanding volume can provide useful information about market trends, investor mood, and prospective trading opportunities. In this book, we'll look at what trading volume is and how traders may utilize it to make trading decisions.

Trading volume is the total number of shares, contracts, or units of an asset purchased and sold in a certain period of time. It is a measure of the level of activity in a specific market or asset and can be studied in a variety of ways, the most frequent being volume-by-timeframe and volume-by-price.

Volume by timeframe

Volume by timeframe displays a security's trading volume over a given time period. It entails plotting a security's trading volume across certain time intervals, such as minutes, hours, days, weeks, or months, rather than just presenting the overall volume for the whole trading session.

On a volume-by-timeframe chart, each bar represents a distinct time interval, and its height indicates the volume traded during that interval. The bars are typically color-coded to represent the level of buying and selling activity. The chart is usually positioned below the price chart, although it can also be layered on top of it.

Volume by Price

Volume by price, also known as volume-at-price or volume profile, is a metric that shows the trading volume of a securities at various price levels. It entails graphing the total volume of an asset traded at each price level, as opposed to merely displaying the overall volume for the whole trading session.

On a volume-by-price chart, each bar represents a specific price level, and its height indicates the volume traded at that level. The bars are typically color-coded to represent the level of buying and selling activity. The chart is usually displayed on the right side of the price chart, either as a distinct chart or as an overlay.

Volume Buying and Selling Climaxes

Buying climax

Buying climax, also known as blow-off, occurs at market peaks when prices suddenly begin to rally quickly after a sustained gain, accompanied by a substantial increase in trading activity, and then peak abruptly. The buying climax candle typically closes toward the center or bottom of the candle. It is a good short-selling opportunity, and the high of the buying climax candle will provide strong resistance.

Selling climax

The selling climax happens when prices begin to fall significantly after a sustained decline, accompanied by a significant increase in trading activity, and then bottom abruptly. The selling climax candle is frequently located in the middle or top of the candle. It is an excellent buying opportunity, and the low of the selling climax candle will provide solid support.

Crucial points to better understand trading volume:

Trading volume might vary significantly based on the type of security being traded.

- For example, high-volume stocks like Apple may have millions of shares moved on any given day, whereas a low-volume instrument like a bond or commodity may see only a few thousand trades in the same time period.
- The time of day or week when trading takes place can also have an impact on trading volume:

Many traders choose to trade during standard market hours, which typically last from 9:30 a.m. to 4:00 p.m. EST, although others may trade after hours or during pre-market hours. Volume can also vary by day of the week, with Mondays and Fridays often having lower trading activity than Tuesdays through Thursdays.

- Other market circumstances and events can affect trading volume:

A significant increase in trading volume, for example, could be caused by a major news event or earnings announcement, whilst a decrease in volume could indicate a lack of investor interest or confidence in a specific security or the market as a whole.

- Volume is only one of several measures that traders and analysts use to assess market activity and trends:

It is crucial to note that trading volume is only one of the numerous measures used by traders and analysts to assess market activity and trends. Other major indicators include price changes, market breadth, and market momentum, all of which can provide useful information about the market's current and future health.

As you can see, trade volume is a complicated and multifaceted subject that requires a detailed understanding to be properly studied and used. Taking the time to delve deeper into its many components and variables allows traders and analysts to obtain a more complete and accurate understanding of the markets and the opportunities they bring.

Chapter 2

Importance of Trading Volume in Investment

Trading volume is a crucial element in investing and trading that is frequently missed by new investors and novice trader. It refers to the quantity of shares or contracts traded over a given time period.

Trading volume is a crucial indication of market activity that can be used to determine how market movements affect trade dates. Understanding the relevance of trading volume can help investors make more educated decisions and increase their chances of success in the stock market or any other market.

Trading volume can be utilized as a technical analysis tool to uncover market trends and patterns. High trading volume typically implies an increase in demand for a specific security, which might result in a price increase.

In contrast, low trading volume can suggest a lack of interest in a security, causing its price to fall. Analyzing trade volume allows investors to spot prospective opportunities and make informed decisions about when to buy or sell a specific security.

Trading volume can also be used to determine the liquidity of an investment. Highly liquid securities can be easily traded in the market, whereas illiquid securities cannot. Liquidity is crucial because it determines how easily an investor can purchase or sell a security. Good trading volume typically indicates good liquidity, which means that investors can buy and sell a security without altering its price.

Reasons why trade volume is crucial in investing

Identifying Market Trends

As previously stated, high trading volume can signal increased demand for a specific asset, resulting in a price increase. Analyzing trade volume allows investors to understand market patterns and make informed decisions about when to buy or sell a specific security.

Assessing liquidity

Trading volume is an important indicator of a security's liquidity. As stated before, good trading volume typically indicates good liquidity, which means that investors can buy and sell a security without altering its price.

Confirming price movement

Trading volume might also help to corroborate price fluctuations. For example, a quick surge in price and trading volume may suggest that the security is in high demand.

Volume shows the level of market activity, which helps price discovery. Increased trading volume frequently accompanies substantial price fluctuations, allowing investors to spot trends and make informed decisions.

Trading volume confirms price patterns. Rising prices and large volume imply strong purchasing demand, which supports positive tendencies. Conversely, dropping prices with heavy volume indicate significant selling pressure, confirming bearish patterns.

Identifying Potential Opportunities

Analyzing trading volume allows investors to spot prospective market opportunities. For example, a sudden spike in trading volume may signal that there is a lot of interest in the securities, resulting in a price increase.

Entry and Exit

It enables traders to understand the moment of entry and exit for a specific investment. Technical analysis is a useful tool for identifying entry and exit opportunities, allowing for maximum profit while minimizing losses. To provide firm confirmation, standard approaches for this type of analysis, such as Moving Average Convergence Divergence (MACD) or Relative Strength Index (RSI), are paired with volume.

Market depth

Volume reflects market depth, indicating the number of participants and the intensity of trading activity. Deep markets with high volume provide more stability and transparency, which attracts more investors.

Volatility Measurement:

Volume helps to measure market volatility. Sharp price changes with significant volume indicate greater volatility and potential trading opportunities. In contrast, low volume during stable periods could imply consolidation or a lack of interest.

Identifying breakouts

Breakouts happen when prices exceed established support or resistance levels. High volume during breakouts verifies price movements and signals future trend reversals or continuations.

Confirmation of Reversals

Volume validates reversal patterns like head and shoulders and double tops/bottoms. An increase in volume during reversal patterns amplifies the signal, implying a larger likelihood of trend reversals.

Divergence Analysis:

Differences between price fluctuations and trade volume can provide useful information.

For example, a price increase combined by diminishing volume may indicate deteriorating momentum, warning against optimistic holdings.

Risk management

Risk management involves monitoring volume to assess market participation and potential liquidity difficulties. Abnormally low volume or rapid surges may signal market disruptions or bad events, necessitating risk mitigation methods.

Investor sentiment:

Volume measures investor mood and market psychology. High volume during market rallies implies optimism and confidence, whereas high volume during declines indicates fear or panic.

Understanding emotion allows investors to better judge market circumstances and change their tactics accordingly.

Trading volume is an important notion in investing that can be used to assess how market changes affect trade dates. Understanding the relevance of trading volume allows investors to make more informed decisions and increase their chances of success in any market.

Chapter 3

Factors affecting trading volume

When examining trading volume, it is critical to evaluate the elements that may influence it. As stated previously, trading volume refers to the number of shares or contracts exchanged in a specific market during a given time period. It is an important statistic for traders and investors to analyze a security's liquidity and predict market direction. Several factors can influence trade volume, and recognizing them is essential for successful trading.

Economic Indicators:

Economic factors such as GDP, inflation rate, and consumer confidence have a considerable impact on trade volume.

For example, a high GDP growth rate may lead to increased expenditure, resulting in larger trading volume. On the other side, high inflation rates might lead to a decline in trading volume since investors may be hesitant to invest in a risky market.

News and events:

News and events like mergers and acquisitions, political events, and earnings releases can all have an impact on trade volume. For example, if a firm publishes higher than expected results, trading volume may increase as investors become more optimistic about the company's future prospects. Conversely, political upheaval or uncertainty might reduce trade volume since investors may be afraid to participate in such a market.

Market Volatility:

Market volatility has a big impact on trade volume. When the market is turbulent, investors may be more likely to trade in order to profit from price swings. Furthermore, excessive volatility might result in greater trading volume as investors attempt to hedge their positions and limit their risk.

Market structure:

The market structure might also have an impact on trading volumes. For example, the existence of high-frequency traders can lead to greater trading volume because they use high-frequency trading tactics, which involve buying and selling at a quick speed.

Several factors can influence trading volume, and understanding them is critical to successful trading. Traders and investors can make informed judgments and successfully manage risk by taking into account economic data, news and events, market volatility, and market structure.

Investor participation:

The level of investor engagement, which includes institutional investors, retail traders, and algorithmic trading systems, influences trading volume. Increased engagement from major institutional investors or high-frequency traders might cause a surge in trading volumes.

Market liquidity:

Liquidity conditions have an impact on trade volume, with liquid markets often seeing higher volumes. Markets with high liquidity promote seamless transactions and attract additional traders, resulting in prolonged trading activity.

Marketing Trends:

Trading volume patterns are influenced by market trends, whether bullish or bearish. Bull markets frequently witness growing trading volumes as investors seek upward price moves, but bear markets may see greater volumes due to selling pressure and profit-taking.

Regulatory changes:

Changes in market regulations, such as trading boundaries, circuit breakers, and transaction charges, can have an impact on trade volumes. Regulatory initiatives aimed at improving market stability or reducing excessive speculation may affect trading dynamics and volume.

Marketing Psychology:

Investor psychology and behavioral biases influence trading volume. Fear, greed, and herd behavior can cause changes in trading volume because investors react emotionally to market conditions and perceived opportunities or risks.

Market exuberance:

Increased trading volumes can occur during periods of market euphoria, when investors are overly optimistic and irrationally enthusiastic about the possibility of making a profit.

Market microstructure:

Trading volume is affected by the market's microstructure, which includes bid-ask spreads, order execution systems, and market-making operations. Market microstructure changes might affect trading behavior and volume patterns.

Government policies:

Government policies, such as fiscal and monetary measures, can have an impact on trading volume because they affect investor confidence, interest rates, and economic conditions. Policy announcements and interventions may cause variations in trade volume.

Global events:

Global events, such as geopolitical tensions, natural disasters, and pandemics, can have a considerable impact on trading volumes. Uncertainty or disruptions caused by global events may increase trading activity as investors modify their portfolios in reaction to changing conditions.

Market Accessibility:

Trading volume is affected by the accessibility of market access, which includes factors such as trading hours, transaction fees, and account requirements. Markets that are more accessible to a wider spectrum of investors typically have larger trading volumes.

Technological Advances:

Technological innovations such as algorithmic trading, high-frequency trading, and electronic trading platforms have altered market dynamics and trading volumes. Automated trading systems can execute huge numbers of trades fast, hence increasing overall trading activity.

Seasonal factors:

Trading volume can be influenced by seasonal trends and patterns in certain markets. For example, the stock market may see increased trading volumes at the start and end of the year due to year-end portfolio adjustments and tax considerations.

Market Speculation:

Speculative behavior, such as investors seeking short-term returns or using momentum trading tactics, can have an impact on trade volume. Speculative bubbles or frenzies may cause volume surges, followed by abrupt corrections.

Chapter 4

Volume Trading Strategies

Volume is a critical indication for numerous trading methods. Here are few examples:

Support and Resistance Levels:

Support and resistance levels are critical price levels where an asset typically bounces or breaks through. By evaluating trading activity at these important levels, traders can evaluate whether there is sufficient buying or selling pressure to break through a level. The amount of trading volume at a support or resistance level may signal that it will hold or break.

Breakout and Breakdown:

Breakout and breakdown trading strategies rely on trading volume to detect future price movements outside of a security's current trading range. When a security's price breaks through a critical level, such as a resistance level, with a large trading volume, it may indicate a breakout or trend reversal. Conversely, if a security's price goes through a critical support level with heavy trading volume, it may indicate a breakdown or downtrend.

Trend Strength:

Trading volume can also help to determine the strength of a trend. For example, a trend accompanied by high trading volume is often regarded as more dependable than one accompanied by low trading volume.

High trading volume in an uptrend can suggest strong purchasing pressure, whereas high trading volume in a decline can indicate strong selling pressure. Traders can utilize trade volume to confirm the strength of a trend and make better trading selections.

Volume Divergence:

Volume divergence is a trading approach that relates price movements to variations in trading volume. If the price of a securities rises as trading volume falls, it may indicate that the trend is losing steam and a reversal is near. If the price falls while trading volume rises, it may imply a trend reversal or breakout is imminent.

Volume Reversal:

Volume reversal is a trading technique that seeks a sharp increase in trading volume following a prolonged period of low volume trading. This abrupt surge in volume, as traders begin to enter or abandon positions, may suggest a trend reversal or breakout. Traders who employ this method often search for a spike in trading volume that is much more than the normal volume for a given security.

These are just a few of the trading systems that use trading volume as a crucial signal when making trade decisions. Trading volume by itself isn't always a good sign, but when used with other technical and fundamental analysis tools, it can tell you a lot about market trends and price changes.

How to Measure Trading Volume

In trading, measuring trading volume is critical for understanding market behavior. Trading volume refers to the number of shares or contracts traded in a specific security or market over a given time period. It is a critical aspect in determining an asset's liquidity and the level of interest from traders and investors. Trading volume can indicate whether a market is trending upwards or downwards.

Technical analysts consider high trade volumes as a favorable sign for a market or security. It shows that there is a lot of interest among traders, and there's a good chance the market will follow the trend. Conversely, low trade volumes can indicate that a market is losing momentum. Technical analysts utilize trading volume to identify critical support and resistance levels that can be used as trade entry and exit points.

Fundamental analysts can use trade volumes to gain useful insights on the health of a firm or sector. A large trading volume for a company's stock may suggest that it is gaining attention from investors and traders, which could be due to favorable news or developments. A low trading volume, on the other hand, may indicate that investors and traders are losing interest, which could be an indication of deeper issues.

Details on trading volume measurement:

Volume Based Indicators

Volume-based indicators are technical indicators that assess market activity and detect future trends and price changes. *Here are some popular volume indicators:*

On-Balance Volume (OBV):

On-Balance Volume (OBV) is a popular volume indicator that quantifies buying and selling pressure by adding or removing volume based on whether the price closes higher or lower than the previous day. It can be used to verify trends and identify potential reversals.

Chaikin Cash Flow (CMF):

The CMF oscillator evaluates buying and selling pressure by examining both price and volume data. It can help to validate patterns and identify potential breakouts.

Volume weighted average price (VWAP):

VWAP is a moving average that accounts for both price and volume data. It is frequently used by institutional traders to calculate the average price at which a stock trades throughout the day.

Accumulation and Distribution Line (ADL):

ADL is a volume and price-based indicator that measures buying and selling pressure. It can be used to confirm trends and predict reversals.

Money Flow Index:

MFI is a momentum indicator that measures buying and selling pressure by analyzing both price and volume. It can be used to spot probable reversals and overbought/oversold situations.

Volume Rate of Change (VROC)

The VROC oscillator measures the rate at which trading volume changes over a given time period. It can help to validate patterns and identify potential breakouts.

These volume-based indicators can provide useful insights into market behavior, allowing traders to make better informed decisions. However, they must be used in conjunction with other technical indicators and fundamental research to avoid false signals and significant losses.

Chapter 5

Trading Volume tips for Swing and Day Traders

Trading volume is an important feature of the trading market since it determines the number of shares or contracts moved in a certain time period. It is a key indicator of market liquidity that counts the number of buyers and sellers in a specific asset.

Understanding trading volume might assist swing and day traders to make better decisions while executing trades. Knowing how to assess trading volume is vital for determining market mood, identifying patterns, and forecasting price moves.

There are various trading volume tips for swing and day traders, and this chapter covers the most effective ones.

Trading Volume tips for Day Traders

Look for strong trading volumes:

Day traders should focus on stocks or securities with significant trading volume. High trading volumes imply that the stock or security is actively traded, which increases the likelihood of executing trades at the target price. Stocks with low trading volumes can experience increased volatility and wider bid-ask spreads, making it difficult to enter and exit deals at the appropriate price.

Analyze intraday volume patterns.

Day traders should look at intraday volume patterns to gauge market sentiment and detect trends.

For example, an increase in trading volume may suggest a positive trend. On the other hand, falling trading volume may suggest a bearish trend.

Use trade volume in combination with technical indicators

Day traders should combine trading volume with technical indicators like moving averages, the relative strength index (RSI), and moving average convergence divergence (MACD). Technical indicators can provide information about the market price fluctuations, while trading volume can confirm or contradict the signals provided by the indicators.

Monitor news and events:

Day traders should be aware of news and events that may have an impact on trading volumes. For example, an earnings report, a merger announcement, or a significant news event can cause a surge in trading volume, signaling heightened volatility in the stock.

Identify abnormal trading volume:

Day traders must identify unusual trading volume. Abnormal trading volume may signal that significant market participants are entering or departing positions. For example, a sudden increase in trading volume may signal that a major player is buying or selling, causing a shift in market sentiment.

Day traders must grasp how to analyze trading volume in order to make sound trading decisions. Day traders can increase their chances of success in the market by looking for high trading volume, evaluating intraday volume trends, combining trading volume with technical indicators, watching news and events, and spotting abnormal trading volume.

Trading Volume Tips for Swing Traders

Volume Analysis of Entry and Exit:

Volume analysis is a key component of successful swing trading. When contemplating entry points, look for substantial volume to accompany price movements, which indicates strong market involvement and increases the chance of a long-term trend. Similarly, consider volume when developing exit strategies.

A drop in volume as the price near your goal level may indicate waning interest among market participants, urging you to consider closing your trade to lock in profits.

Identify volume patterns.

Dive deeper into volume patterns to find hidden opportunities. Volume spikes, for example, frequently occur in conjunction with important market events or news releases, providing useful insights into market sentiment and probable price direction. Furthermore, look for accumulation or distribution periods that are marked by sustained purchasing or selling pressure over time, as these might predict large price moves.

Focus on liquid stocks or pairs

Liquidity is required to execute swing trades efficiently. Liquid equities with high trading volume have tighter spreads and lower slippage, which reduces transaction costs and mitigates the impact of market orders. Focusing on liquid equities allows you to join and exit positions more effortlessly, this could improve your trading results.

Volume Confirmation:

Use volume confirmation to validate your trading signals and improve the consistency of your swing trades. For example, if you see a bullish chart pattern emerging, such as a cup and handle, look for a commensurate increase in volume during the breakout over the handle's resistance level.

This volume confirmation strengthens your trading strategy, increasing the likelihood of a favorable outcome.

Volume Surge at Breakouts:

Pay special attention to volume surges that accompany breakout moves, since they frequently mark the start of new trends. High-volume breakouts signal strong buying or selling pressure, which confirms the breakout's authenticity and provides excellent swing trading possibilities. Look for persistent volume expansion after the breakout to confirm the new trend's strength.

Volume Divergence:

Volume divergences can serve as early indicators of probable trend reversals or exhaustion. For example, if you find prices reaching new highs but volume falls, it could imply diminishing bullish momentum and an eventual reversal. Similarly, falling prices on increased volume may indicate distribution by institutional investors and presage a decline. Incorporating volume divergence analysis into your swing trading technique allows you to anticipate market trends and change your positions accordingly.

Volume Confirmation for Pullbacks:

During pullback settings, volume confirmation can help differentiate between transitory retracements and trend reversals.

A drop in volume during a pullback indicates a lack of selling pressure, implying that the current trend is intact. In contrast, a jump in volume during pullback may indicate increasing selling activity and the possibility of a trend reversal. Analyzing volume trends during pullbacks allows you to make better decisions about whether to enter, hold, or exit swing trades.

Volume at the Support and Resistance levels:

Volume analysis at key support and resistance levels gives useful information about market mood and price behavior. High-volume breakdowns of support or resistance levels are more likely to result in big price changes, which provide good swing trading opportunities. Also, note how volume reacts when the price approaches certain levels. Increasing volume when the price approaches a support/resistance level indicates growing market confidence, increasing the likelihood of a successful breakout or reversal.

Volume Patterns for Consolidation:

Consolidation phases frequently precede major price movements in swing trading. Monitor volume patterns during consolidation periods to predict potential breakout or breakdown moves.

Increasing volume during consolidation shows that institutional investors or significant market participants are accumulating or distributing shares, signaling that market sentiment is about to move.

By examining volume dynamics as well as price movement, you can position yourself to profit from rising trends after consolidation.

Stay informed about news events:

Market news and events can have a significant impact on trading volume and sentiment, affecting the result of swing trades. Keep track of forthcoming earnings releases, economic reports, and geopolitical occurrences that may impact market dynamics. Anticipating fluctuations in trading activity caused by news events allows you to alter your swing trading strategy accordingly, reducing risk and increasing rewards.

Advantages and disadvantages of analyzing trading volume

The advantages

There are various benefits to monitoring trading volume data, whether for an individual security or the larger market.

- Monitoring liquidity and investor interest in a certain security.
- Confirming price trend strength.
- Detecting reversals earlier.
- Observing odd activity.
- Evaluating the overall health of the market.

The disadvantages

While insightful, traders should be mindful of the following limitations before depending only on trading volume:

- Prediction power is limited.
- Averages may vary greatly among securities.
- It is susceptible to manipulation, particularly when the market is highly illiquid or prices are excessively low.

Volume analysis has the maximum influence when paired with other technical and fundamental considerations.

- Unusual volume spikes can be generated using dubious methods such as pump-and-dump procedures.

Thus, trade volumes should not be the main factor influencing trading decisions.

Chapter 6

Summary

Trading Volume: Key to Success

When it comes to successful trading, numerous things might influence the outcome of a transaction. One such aspect is trading volume, which refers to the number of shares or contracts traded during a given period of time. Trading volume can have a substantial impact on the success of a trade since it influences market liquidity, asset values, and general market movements.

Liquidity:

One of the most important ways in which trade volume influences effective trading is through its impact on market liquidity.

When trade volume is high, there are more buyers and sellers in the market, making it easier to purchase or sell an item at a reasonable price. This is especially crucial for traders who need to enter or leave positions quickly, since limited liquidity can cause slippage and greater trading expenses.

Price movements:

Another way that trade volume influences effective trading is through its effect on asset values. When trading volume is large, it can produce market momentum, causing prices to rise or fall based on the overall emotion of the traders. By studying trading volume data, traders can obtain insight into market movements and make informed judgments about whether to enter or quit a position.

Confirmation:

Trading volume can also be used to support or dispute other technical indicators. For example, if a trader notices a bullish candlestick pattern on a chart, they may wish to validate that mood by examining trading volume data. If the trading volume is likewise strong, it might provide further confirmation that market sentiment is optimistic and that now is a good time to begin a long position.

Risk Management:

Finally, trade volume might impact risk management. Low trading volume makes it difficult to leave a position quickly, increasing the chance of loss.

By tracking trading volume data, traders can identify possible liquidity concerns and change their trading tactics accordingly. For example, if trading volume is low, a trader may wish to cut their position size or refrain from trading altogether until liquidity increases.

Trading volume is an important component to consider when determining the success of a trade. Understanding the significance of trading volume in market liquidity, price movements, confirmation, and risk management allows traders to make more educated decisions about when to enter or quit a position. While trading volume should not be the only aspect examined when executing a trade, it can provide useful information to assist traders optimize profits and avoid risks.

Thank you for purchasing this book.

Happy the trading!!

www.ingramcontent.com/pod-product-compliance
Lightning Source LLC
Chambersburg PA
CBHW070414230526
45471CB00006B/2794